Women of Yesterday for Women of Today

Rhonda K. Bello

Women of Yesterday for Women of Today
Copyright © 2015 by Rhonda K. Bello
Kingdom Builders Publications
All rights reserved. No part of this book may be reproduced or transmitted in any form or by any means without written permission from the author.

ISBN: 978-0-6924-0038-8
Library of Congress Control Number: 2015936826

Cover Designer
Cover artwork titled "Faith Hope & Love"
by artist Henry Lee Battle
www.henryleebattle.com
LoMar Designs

Illustrator and Artist Permission by
Henry Lee Battle

Author's Photograph
Bamidele Bello
Editors: Louise Smith

Printed in USA
Go to our website:
www.kingdombuilderspublications.com

Women of Yesterday for Women of Today

Rhonda K. Belle

This Book Belongs

DEDICATION

This book is dedicated to the Almighty God, the creator of the Heavens and Earth; He who inspired me to believe in Him; who kept my faith strong even when the storms of life nearly swallowed me. I dedicate also to the family of Holy Mountain International Ministries (Blessed House) for their support. Continue to believe in Jesus Christ of Nazareth.

CONTENTS

DEDICATION IV
CONTENTS VI
ACKNOWLEDGMENTS 1
CHAPTER ONE 3
EVE: OUR FIRST MOTHER 3
CHAPTER TWO 7
JOB'S WIFE: TOTAL LOSS FOR WORDS 7
CHAPTER THREE 12
ESTHER: GOTTA HAVE FAITH 12
CHAPTER FOUR 17
WOMEN WITH ISSUANCE OF BLOOD: 17
WHAT A BEST DAY 17
CHAPTER FIVE 22
RUTH: FAVOR 22
ABOUT THE AUTHOR 29

ACKNOWLEDGMENTS

This Book is dedicated to The Most High God Almighty who hand crafted me, watches over and paves my destiny continuously. My God has never let me down and can do ANYTHING.

Secondly, my husband Pastor Bamidele Bello was designed by God as my friend, my spiritual advisor and my help mate. He always has a prayer, a word of encouragement and lets me know that he and God are always listening.

I like also like to dedicate to everyone that I have met; was supposed to meet as well as family and friends. Each person was designed to touch my life. God never makes mistakes. Everyone that I have met was for a purpose. It does not matter what the reason God gave them or did not give them; all that matters is it was a reason.

I am not going to say anything negative because God designed us to be positive; nor will I write something bitter because God gave us love. I will not even present a case to be judged because God has concluded everything. I am just glad He gave me the strength when I needed it and the courage when I had to enforce it.

Nobody knows what I felt, but hopefully they will feel what God wants for their design. We are destined to be GREAT. God gives us that opportunity not every day, but every second. Let us stop pretending that we are NOT loved by God.

Rhonda K. Bello

Two passages stand out in the Bible:

Be thankful in all circumstances, for this is God's will for you who belong to Christ Jesus. 1 Thessalonians 5:15 NLT

> ^{1}*Shout for joy to the LORD, all the earth.*
> ^{2} *Worship the LORD with gladness;*
> *come before him with joyful songs.*
> ^{3}*Know that the LORD is God.*
> *It is He who made us, and we are his;*
> *we are his people, the sheep of his pasture.*
> ^{4}*Enter his gates with thanksgiving*
> *and his courts with praise;*
> *give thanks to him and praise his name.*
> ^{5}*For the LORD is good and his love endures forever; his faithfulness continues through all generations.*
> *Psalm 100:1-5 NIV*

Finally, I had never heard of Louise Smith or Kingdom Builders Publications, but God directed us to meet each other. Thank you, thank you my spiritual sister for just being obedient and listening to what our God has directed you to do to build His kingdom. Louise is an inspiration, a heavenly singer and is touched with anointing.

God is good all the time. All the time God is good.

CHAPTER ONE

EVE: OUR FIRST MOTHER

SCRIPTURES
Genesis 2:18-4:26; 2 Corinthians 11:3;
1 Timothy 2:13; Genesis 2:18
Amplified Bible (AMP)

[18]Now the Lord God said, It is not good (sufficient, satisfactory) that the man should be alone; I will make him a helper (suitable, adapted, complementary) for him.

Genesis 4:26 Amplified Bible (AMP)
[26]And to Seth also a son was born, whom he named Enosh. At that time men began to call [upon God] by the name of the Lord.

2 Corinthians 11:3 Amplified Bible (AMP)
[3]But [now] I am fearful, lest that even as the serpent beguiled Eve by his cunning, so your minds may be corrupted and seduced from wholehearted and sincere and pure devotion to Christ.

1 Timothy 2:13 Amplified Bible (AMP)
[13]For Adam was first formed, then Eve;

Rhonda K. Belle

Featured Scriptures Verse

Genesis 2:23
"At last!" the man exclaimed.
"This one is bone from my bone,
and flesh from my flesh!
She will be called 'woman,'
because she was taken from 'man.'" (NLT)

The scriptures do not mention much about Eve but from what God has revealed to us is very important or it would not have been written.

First Woman, Wife, Mother, and first female pioneer.

She is the mother of all the living creatures. Woman came from man but from that day forth, man came from the female. That lets us know that we are vital to God for creation. We should always use our bodies as temples.

Adam's companion, his helper, the one who would complete him and share equally in his responsibility over creation was hand crafted by God from Adam himself. Only together they could fulfill God's purpose in the continuation of creation. Not to say that man was the first living thing but ever since then, man had to come to this earth through a woman. With Eve, God brought human relationship, friendship, and marriage into the world.

She was specially designed from Adam to be his help mate. She is the only woman that has no mother or father. From her being deceived by Satan, the woman had to endure a lot and this fact remains even today. This is where we need to pause; Eve lost sight of her faith to trust only God. Women….we have to stand firm in our faith. Eve had the best relationship with God but she did not understand the precious gift she had. God still talks to us individually. And if we are so very favored that God will use us to the ultimate, then we never EVER betray Him. Now when Eve did eat the fruit from the forbidden tree, she invited her husband Adam to enjoy the taste of the "eye opening" fruit. Eve blamed Satan because she got entangled in his deceptive trap. We are individually made with choices. If we decide that we do not want to obey God, or honor our helpmate (the one that God personally chose for us), do not blame anyone but ourselves when your consequences brings to a spiral end.

APPLICATION

We are vital to God. Our bodies should always be considered holy temples. We should not defile our bodies by fad piercings, creating health problems by obesity, using the body as a sex tool or even posing in compromising pictures.

We should always walk as the Lord has told us. We are princesses and queens because Jesus Christ is our King. We are highly favored because God took his time and made us out of his own image. Every step we take we are walking in God's grace and favor. We are his tangible testimonies. Continue to be blessed.

PRAYER

God continue to bless me abundantly and I pray that the Heavens will open up to give me scandalous testimonies.
God use me. I give myself away to you.
My Lord, my God, you can do anything but lie. I have no power on my own. Bless me now.
In Jesus Name Amen.

DECREE

I decree and declare our God will lead you on your journey to amazing discoveries.
I decree and declare that our Lord will raise you and your family above to higher ground.

CHAPTER TWO

JOB'S WIFE: TOTAL LOSS FOR WORDS

ᗡ(SCRIPTURE)ᗞ

His wife said to him, "Are you still maintaining your integrity? Curse God and die!" Job 2:9 NIV

This particular woman did not have a name. Her name was not the relevance to the story but her actions and her understanding were. If you don't know the story, she was NOT supportive towards her husband. She wanted Job to curse God and die. She did not portray elements of a good Christian Woman.

We should sympathize and understand that Job's wife lost just as much her spouse. She lost her social status, family, servants, workers and cattle. She was instantly in poverty. She was not prepped or prepared for instant disaster. She did not have an briefing or a study session. This particular morning, she woke up with no worries but by nightfall of the SAME day, she's now going to bed trying to figure out how and from where will they eat the next day.

Job's wife is in the Bible as a tool for us to use. We need to understand that God wants us to stand strong regardless of the weather. We are not guaranteed good days forever but everlasting life. We are not guaranteed to be top of our social status but to be front runners for God. We are not guaranteed mortal bliss but spiritual fulfillment in every area of our lives. We're not guaranteed not to cry, but when we do cry; know that God is the God of ALL comfort in the Holy Spirit.

APPLICATION

We as women do not understand that we are made from man's "his" rib. We need him just as much as he need us. When that significant male wants to give up and quit, women, our role is to push him forward. Sometimes it requires being silent while the male goes forward for the light. We must comprehend that we are the *helpmate*. Once we have taken our marriage to the Lord, then the Lord can work on our behalf. Taking our marriage is not just a one-time thing, but this is required daily; several times even if need be.

Studying the Bible together will increase you and your spouse. Then when you are confronted with woes and trouble, you will feel the solid foundation in living as a Christian Woman. It can challenging living as a Christian Woman, but changing your way of thinking will help greatly. The Bible says that the way of the transgressor is hard. He makes our burdens light and our yokes easy. There is not a test, or essay or even a step by Now while there is not step manual on how to live as a Christian Women, God's word is the final authority and all of our situations are answered in the Living Word of God. We are blessed because God has made provisions in Proverbs and throughout the Bible to govern us.

Proverbs 31:10-31 (KJV)

[10] *Who can find a virtuous woman? for her price is far above rubies.*

[11] *The heart of her husband doth safely trust in her, so that he shall have no need of spoil.*

[12] *She will do him good and not evil all the days of her life.*

[13] *She seeketh wool, and flax, and worketh willingly with her hands.*

[14] *She is like the merchants' ships; she bringeth her food from afar.*

[15] *She riseth also while it is yet night, and giveth meat to her household, and a portion to her maidens.*

[16] *She considereth a field, and buyeth it: with the fruit of her hands she planteth a vineyard.*

[17] *She girdeth her loins with strength, and strengtheneth her arms.*

¹⁸ She perceiveth that her merchandise is good: her candle goeth not out by night.
¹⁹ She layeth her hands to the spindle, and her hands hold the distaff.
²⁰ She stretcheth out her hand to the poor; yea, she reacheth forth her hands to the needy.
²¹ She is not afraid of the snow for her household: for all her household are clothed with scarlet.
²² She maketh herself coverings of tapestry; her clothing is silk and purple.
²³ Her husband is known in the gates, when he sitteth among the elders of the land.
²⁴ She maketh fine linen, and selleth it; and delivereth girdles unto the merchant.
²⁵ Strength and honour are her clothing; and she shall rejoice in time to come.
²⁶ She openeth her mouth with wisdom; and in her tongue is the law of kindness.
²⁷ She looketh well to the ways of her household, and eateth not the bread of idleness.
²⁸ Her children arise up, and call her blessed; her husband also, and he praiseth her.
²⁹ Many daughters have done virtuously, but thou excellest them all.
³⁰ Favour is deceitful, and beauty is vain: but a woman that feareth the LORD, she shall be praised.
³¹ Give her of the fruit of her hands; and let her own works praise her in the gates.

PRAYER

Dear Lord, help us to live as a Christian woman, mother, sister, aunt, grandmother, niece and friend.

My God, reveal your purpose to me and unleash the gifts in me so I may do your work.
In Jesus Name Amen.

⊃(DECREE)⊂

I decree and declare our God will only have your tongue to speak prosperity for your spirit, soul and body.
I decree and declare that our Lord will raise you above and you will stand as the example of a Christian Woman.

CHAPTER THREE

ESTHER: GOTTA HAVE FAITH

Have you ever had a situation come upon you where you had to make a major decision that would ultimately change fate?

Examples:
- Go to work or go to college
- Study hard or just pass
- Volunteer or demand a salary
- Get involved or just play it out to see the outcome
- Miss the first bus and chance catching the second

Pray that the Lord guide your major decisions. Our thought and prayer comes from *Esther 8:3*

And Esther spake yet again before the king, and fell down at his feet, and besought him with tears to put away the mischief of Haman the Agagite, and his device that he had devised against the Jews.

One fine day, King Ahasuerus held a huge banquet for everyone in his kingdom. When Ahasuerus was drunk, he ordered his wife, Queen Vashti, to appear at the banquet wearing her beautiful crown. (Some commentators suggest that this meant that she should wear only her crown!) But Vashti refused. As punishment for Vashti's disobedience, King Ahasuerus banished her from the palace. To choose a new queen, the king called for a beauty pageant and chose Esther. He married her. She kept her Jewish identity a secret on the advice of Mordecai, her uncle.

The king's ministers, Bigthan and Teresh, plotted to kill the king. Mordecai learned of their plot, told Queen Esther, and Esther reported it to the king. The king ordered the two plotters to be hanged. King Ahasuerus then chose Haman as his senior minister. Haman demanded complete loyalty of everyone in the king's service, and ordered all to bow down to him. But Mordecai refused, giving as an excuse that bowing down to another person was forbidden by his Jewish faith. This angered Haman, and he decreed the destruction not only of Mordecai, but of all the Jews the kingdom. To determine the day for carrying out the decree, Haman cast lots, or "purim." The lot fell on the 13th of Adar. News of the decree spread throughout the kingdom, and the Jews were greatly distressed. Mordecai urged Esther to plead with the king to save the lives of her people. Queen Esther summoned all of her courage and went before the king. By using her feminine wiles, Esther persuaded the king to offer her the fulfillment of any wish. She told him about the plot against her people and asked that it be stopped. The king granted her wish and ordered Haman to be hanged In Esther's times, women were seen and never heard. Esther's life was groomed to become the king's wife but that grooming was the outside appearance only. No one but God can change the inside appearance of some one. We have tried ourselves but our abilities pale and we have failed. Once we solicit the help from God through consistent prayer, then and **ONLY** then can we change from inside out.

Esther knew her place and knew the other wife came up missing so she knew in order not to be the next missing wife; she had to deal with a delicate situation. This is where she had her *"sliding*

door moment". Now when we believe in God, we can ONLY have a happy moment.

Through the wisdom of God – Through Christ I can do ALL things – Esther not only made the right decisions but ultimately had the King's eyes open to his surrounding with the helpers he had.

We must remember that the Lord never gives us too much to bear. He holds our future and Jesus paid the price for us.

APPLICATION

We have all come across our journeys as Esther. Let us remember to pray as well as fast as our sister Esther did. Faith unlocks the door to our prayers but we must fast so that the Lord can see our heart. Challenge yourself to fast and pray before you make any decision. Use your faith to unlock the door.

PRAYER

Pray that the Lord guide your major decisions
Pray that the Lord give you helpers
Pray that you have abundance of knowledge in the Lord
Pray that the Lord continue to guide your footsteps and that nothing earth has will contain

you.
We know that earth could not hold Jesus, therefore earth cannot contain your future. Earth will have to give back everything owed to us.
Pray that the Lord will change you inside out.
In Jesus Name Amen.

⚜ DECREE ⚜

I decree and declare that you will lead the people that God has placed in front of you.
I decree and declare that God will never let your well of life run dry.
I decree and declare that God has said Amen over your situation.

CHAPTER FOUR

WOMAN WITH ISSUANCE OF BLOOD: WHAT A BEST DAY

Mark 5:24-34

24 And Jesus went with him; and much people followed him, and thronged him.

25 And a certain woman, which had an issue of blood twelve years,

26 And had suffered many things of many physicians, and had spent all that she had, and was nothing bettered, but rather grew worse,

27 When she had heard of Jesus, came in the press behind, and touched his garment.

28 For she said, If I may touch but his clothes, I shall be whole.

29 And straightway the fountain of her blood was dried up; and she felt in her body that she was healed of that plague.

30 And Jesus, immediately knowing in himself that virtue had gone out of him, turned him about in the press, and said, Who touched my clothes?

31 And his disciples said unto him, Thou seest the multitude thronging thee, and sayest thou, Who touched me?

32 And he looked round about to see her that had done this thing.

33 But the woman fearing and trembling, knowing what was

done in her, came and fell down before him, and told him all the truth.
³⁴And he said unto her, Daughter, thy faith hath made thee whole; go in peace, and be whole of thy plague.

Now let's break down exactly what happened. ...
Suddenly the group in front of her shifted, parting like the waters of the Jordan before the children of promise. It was all she needed. She had a urgency to get to Jesus as the others who thronged and pressed him. Instantly, she felt a warmth like none other penetrating and covering; going through her, flushing out the pain, and clearing out the decay.
That feeling was so different and very noticeable until she knew at that moment she was healed.

This woman had an issuance which the Bible is telling us an "issue" is what we have today. Some of us have an issue with finance, family and marriage, and job relationships. No matter the volume or the secrecy, nevertheless there are issues. How would you feel, if you were to open your mailbox and find a $300,000 check waiting for you? I think you would feel beside myself, surreal, warm, lively and joyous. This is exactly how this woman felt!

Saints, we have to remember that this woman was healed instantly. After she had gone to doctor after doctor spending all her living, she finally went to the right doctor. JESUS. My sisters and brothers, we do the same thing, we run to this doctor, then to that herbalist, then another ministry. Some go to another faith or persuasion instead of running to JESUS. Jesus is the miracle worker. He is the Alpha and Omega. He is the beginning and the end. He knows what we are in need of before we ask, Jesus will be there waiting for us. He would say:

"My daughter, my son, I've have stood at your door of your heart knocking and waiting. Now you let me in. I will give you peace, assurance, joy, rest, blessing, favor, mercy, goodness, greatness. You will hunger no more because I will be feeding you by my word." Once we let Jesus in, we are instantly healed!!

There are two things I want to point out here. They are:
1. The woman's problem
2. The woman's status

We discuss the women's problem but not yet the woman's status. Jesus healed this woman and then instantly change her from a nobody to a somebody. Initially she was just a woman, but after the encounter with Jesus, instantly she became His daughter. Jesus did not mention her by not as *woman* or *sinner*, but as **Daughter**. She was no longer alone, but an excepted part of His family by virtue of her faith. His touch proved to be the more contagious; rendering her pure and whole again. God honors faithfulness.

Hebrews 11:1-2
Now faith is being sure of what we hope for and certain of what we do not see. This is what the ancients were commended for.

Every day I pray for the Lord to strengthen my faith.

APPLICATION

We have been suffering minutes, hours, days, weeks, months and years from different issuances. We need to have faith that once we have carry our issuances to the Lord in prayer, He will hear us, deliver us and set us free. We were healed; we are healed. Can you imagine…just faith can cure you! What are we waiting for? Touch the hem of Jesus' garment now and be healed.

Carrying around an unnecessary issuance is not only tiring but useless. Let us put our faith in the one that is with us 24/7. Let us put Jesus to the test. He can do anything but FAIL.

⁂ PRAYER ⁂

My Lord, please make a way for me, and clear my path so that I may see, feel and be surrounded by your Glory.

Lord, let my faith in You heal me.

Lord, You are the only one that can cure my long issuance of finance, emotional, stress, marital, job, business and any other thing that I have been afflicted.

In Jesus Name. Amen.

⁂ DECREE ⁂

I decree and declare that any long time suffering is healed NOW.

I decree and declare that Jesus is answering my prayers.

I decree and declare that my suffering will stop and not become a generational curse.

CHAPTER FIVE

RUTH: FAVOR

Ruth is proof that God shows us favor. Once I was blessed to hear Bishop Adewale (Wale) Adekoya speak and he gave us a simple recipe for favor. He referenced

Surely goodness and mercy shall follow me every day of my life and I shall dwell in the house of the Lord forever.
Psalm 23:6
In Jesus Name, Amen.

It is a simple recipe. Goodness + Mercy = Favor. God is not difficult. He has given us a recipe. Ruth followed that recipe.

First the goodness that God showed Ruth. Ruth was married to the right man at the right time. That's it!! Sometimes we must go through a training period before we can achieve the gift that God truly has for us. Ruth's training period was her first marriage and the journey with Naomi.

Now goodness never left Ruth because the recipe

calls for both goodness and mercy. Next is mercy. Mercy we know is something that God gives us though we do not deserve it. Ruth's story if viewed deeper, she received mercy because of her humility towards Naomi. Ruth made sure Naomi was cared for and watched over. What Ruth did or didn't do is not the relevance here but the mercy that was shown over her life. The two main ingredients shown here are Goodness plus Mercy.

The sum total of these two components is Favor. Favor was shown when Ruth met and eventually marries Boaz. Through normal chains (human chains), there shouldn't have been any way possible that Ruth could have met Boaz; let alone the thought of marriage. Ruth was so low on the social scale, that if we gave her a number it would start with negative.

One song comes in mind:
"I never knew He would honor me this way, (2),
Honor me this way (2), Thank you Jesus"
That must be the song that she sung when she knew that she would marry Boaz. She is the virtuous woman. God is a GREAT GOD. Here are some key points from Barnes Bible Charts.

Proverbs 31:10
Who can find a virtuous woman? for her price is far above rubies.

Proverbs 12:4
A virtuous woman is a crown to her husband: but she that maketh ashamed is as rottenness in his bones.

Ruth 3:11
And now, my daughter, fear not; I will do to thee all that thou requirest: for all the city of my people doth know that thou art a virtuous woman.

APPLICATION

Have you dreamt of your soul mate, a joyous job or even how many children you would have? Did you know that whatever is spoken here on earth is acknowledged in Heaven? Let your dreams come true. First, trust that God has not only the master plan but the only plan for our life. Love Jesus. God loved so much that He gave us His only begotten Son. Last, we must practice listening to God before we jump into any decisions.

Matthew 18:18 NIV
Truly I tell you, whatever you bind on earth will be bound in heaven, and whatever you loose on earth will be loosed in heaven.

John 3:16 KJV
For God so loved the world, that he gave his only begotten Son,

that whosoever believeth in him should not perish, but have everlasting life.

⚜ PRAYER ⚜

My awesome God, with your goodness and mercy; show me favor.
Mighty God, bless me with abundances of favor.
Lord, my God, talk to me.
In Jesus Name. Amen.

⚜ DECREE ⚜

I decree and declare that everyone under the sound of my voice shall have joy, peace and abundances.
I decree and declare for the obedience you will show to God our Father.

GO IN PEACE AND CONTINUE TO RECEIVE YOUR BLESSING.

ALTAR CALL

After you have read this book and you are questioning your relationship with God and you are not sure if you are saved eternally from sin then I want you to pray this prayer:

Lord, I confess that I am a sinner and today I give myself to you. Lord use me, mold me and teach me to be one of your warriors. Lord, I have no power of my own and I need your help, your guidance, your provision and your safety. Take me Lord under your Shadow and shield me from all hurt, harm and danger. Lord, bless me with mercy, grace and goodness. Lord, let me be your tangible testimony. In Jesus Name. Amen.

Please find a church home where you can give your time, talent and tithes. God gave us talent and we need to give back in order for His glory to be revealed through us.

VOTE OF THANKS

I'd like to first thank God for choosing me as His vessel to print this message. Without Him, we are NOTHING. Next, I like to thank my husband, Pastor Bello, who has given me encouragement throughout my journey in ministry. He had the faith in me when I was still searching for answers. Finally, I would like to thank my family.

My grandmother who started me in New Hope Baptist Church. My fraternal grandmother who started me in believing that everyone I associate with must know Jesus. My sister Jyllene who will basically fought every battle with me. My sister Connie who would come see me even when I was in Zimbabwe. My brother who was the authority head and counselor of the family. My sister Tracy who taught me there is a world outside of the "Lexington Terrace." And finally my adopted mother Sister Rita Davis who has the faith for 10,000 plus people. She is a true tangible testimony that God is REAL.

I have to mention two spiritual leaders in my life. They are a couple that God directed me to for preparation for the long hard journey I had ahead. First, Evangelist Marilyn Johnson: we didn't know initially; but she prepared me for the new role as First Lady. The revelation of her training will be reality for me very soon. Second is Pastor Larry Johnson who preaches realistic sermons. He is a preacher that understands that a saint once had a past whether good or bad. I thank them from the bottom of my heart and will continue to pray that God keeps fresh anointing on their head and the windows of Heaven will continue to shower down abundantly.

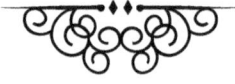

ABOUT THE AUTHOR

Minister Rhonda Bello is a Maryland native and loves the Lord, education, reading as well as teaching. She retired 2011 from the United States Army where she served over 24 years of faithful service. She is now less than 1 year from receiving her Doctorate Degree in Business in Administration from University of Phoenix. Rhonda holds her MA in accounting from University of Phoenix. She is in the executive board for a NGO agency, Global Organization for Humanitarian Relief as the Legal Advisor, certified with IRS to perform services for tax preparation, a mentor with University of Phoenix Mentorship Program, University of Maryland Mentorship Program, America Corporate Partners (ACP) Protégé program and Business and Professional Women Foundation (BPW). Rhonda is District 27 Toastmasters Chaplain. Rhonda is also University of Phoenix Alumni District of Columbia President. She is co-founder and currently works as the Assistant Pastor at Holy Mountain International Ministries.

Rhonda Bello has also written an endorsement for a book which will release in 2015. She was also a contributing author in the book called, **You are called to Greatness**. Her first book was publish March 2015 entitled **Women of Yesterday for Women of Today.**

As a transformational leader and the faith of prayer, Rhonda's future endeavors include helping expand Prayer and Salvation Organization to different parts of the world and leaving the knowledge of what prayer can do in each and everyone's lives. Rhonda will incorporate private consulting for revivals, power lunches and also educational services for starting churches. The Prayer and Salvation Organization have joined the Aderaf Investments, LLC international business.

She believes that the people calls impossible are possible with God. Her favorite theorists are Taylor (1911) who states we must work smarter not harder. Maslow (1943) who describes the hierarchy of needs is her other favorite theorist. The Bible states in the book of (Romans 13:8) "We should owe nothing but love" and that is what she lives by every day. Every day is the best day of her life.

Women of Yesterday for Women of Today

Contact Information
Rhonda Bello Ministries
Rhonda.bello1@gmail.com
443-367-1951

References

All Scripture quotes are from the King James Version of the Bible with the exception of these

Retrieved on 1 December 2015 from
http://www.womeninthebible.net

Retrieved on 1 December 2015 from
http://www.biblestudytools.com   author David Peach

Retrieved on 1 December 2015 from
https://www.biblegateway.com/passage/

Retrieved on 1 December 2015 from
http://www.whatchristianswanttoknow.com

Retrieved on 1 December 2015 from http://www.israel-a-history-of.com/queen-esther-of-the-bible.html

Retrieved on 1 December 2015 from
http://www.sermoncentral.com/sermons/scripture/sermons-on-esther-1.asp   author Ann Spangler and Jean Syswerda Bible

*Bishop Wale Adekoya found on
Chapter 5 p. 22
Quote from
Principles of Walking in Divine Favour
Flowing in the River of Favour

Women of Yesterday for Women of Today

Yesterday's Women

Women Today